AMPHETAMINES AND OTHER STIMULANTS

Stimulants are a major part of the drug problem in America.

AMPHETAMINES AND OTHER STIMULANTS

Lawrence Clayton, Ph.D.

THE ROSEN PUBLISHING GROUP, INC.
NEW YORK

To Annette Colbert, a friend.

The people pictured in this book are only models; they in no way practice or endorse the activities illustrated. Captions serve only to explain the subjects of the photographs and do not imply a connection between real-life models and the staged situations shown. News agency photographs are exceptions.

Published in 1994 by The Rosen Publishing Group, Inc.
29 East 21st Street, New York, NY 10010

Copyright 1994 by The Rosen Publishing Group, Inc.

First Edition

Printed in Canada

Library of Congress Cataloging-in-Publication Data

Clayton, L. (Lawrence)
        Amphetamines and other stimulants / by Lawrence
        Clayton.
        p.   cm.— (The Drug abuse prevention library)
        Includes bibliographical references and index.
                ISBN 0-8239-1534-4
                1. Amphetamines—Juvenile literature. 2.
                Stimulants—Juvenile literature. 3. Drug abuse—
                United States—Juvenile literature. [1. Amphet-
                amines. 2. Drug abuse.] I. Title. II. Series.
                HV5822.A5C53   1994
                362.29'9—dc20   94-573
                                                                    CIP
                                                                    AC

Contents

Stimulant abuse can lead to serious medical problems.

CHAPTER 1

Stimulants, Their Use and Abuse

*A*mphetamines have a very unusual history. They are a drug that almost didn't get to be a drug. In fact, no one could find a use for them for almost 50 years after they were discovered. Then they were found helpful in treating several medical problems, from low blood pressure to depression. After that, no new use for amphetamines and other stimulants has ever been found.

During World War II (1939-45), the British, American, Italian, Japanese, and German soldiers were given stimulants to help them stay awake and be more alert. The soldiers soon discovered that they had more energy as well. The drugs became a part of many soldiers' regular supplies.

8   As far as we know, it was American soldiers who first began to abuse stimulants.
It happened in Korea in 1953. A group of
addicts were running low on heroin. So
they mixed amphetamine with heroin and
discovered that the high was more intense
than with heroin alone.

Beginning of Abuse

By the early 1960s, amphetamine abuse
was a major problem among the young. It
was during this period that the drugs were
first called "speed." This was because they
speed up the user's body. They increase
heart, pulse, and breathing rate. They also
cause the user to stay awake, lose weight,
and be more alert. They also cause users
to develop acne (pimples) and boils, especially on the face.

Amphetamines were originally prescribed by doctors. But hospitals and
doctors began reporting many serious
problems. Young people were suffering
from heart attacks and strokes, which
were very unusual for this age group.
Doctors and pharmacists noticed that
young people were forging prescriptions
for stimulants. Also, more teenagers were
becoming addicted to these drugs.

Doctors began to place tighter limits on the amounts of stimulants they prescribed. The police began to crack down on drug-stores that sold the drugs illegally.

Speed Labs

Soon illegal "speed labs" sprang up on the West Coast. This had many serious consequences. Prescription stimulants were of high quality because the drug companies were controlled by federal law.

There were no such controls for the illegal labs. Many of them were dirty, did not use trained chemists, and used whatever chemicals they could find. Soon hundreds of young people were showing up at hospitals sick, dying or dead, from drugs that were incorrectly made.

Before long, young people in California found out that mixing heroin with stimulants gave them an unusually intense high. They named this powerful combination a "speedball."

Crystal-Meth

Meanwhile, back at the illegal labs, chemists had begun to combine amphetamine and Methedrine. This combination was very dangerous to make, but it gave

10 | the users the most intense high they had ever experienced. Soon, thousands of young people were abusing this new drug, called methamphetamine or crystal-meth.

By 1971, so many people were addicted to stimulants that the United States strictly limited the amounts that doctors could prescribe. This caused the speed labs to spread across the country. Soon they were in almost every state.

Both truck drivers and airplane pilots found that using stimulants enabled them to drive and fly for much longer periods. They began calling the drugs "copilots." This use has a side problem, however. Sometimes the user becomes unconscious for a while. This caused so many accidents that very strict laws were passed forbidding stimulant use while driving a truck or flying a plane.

Stimulants are still a major problem for young people. The latest studies show that around 20 percent of high school seniors have used stimulants. About 11 percent of them are addicted.

Many others have used stimulants believing that they were using cocaine. It is thought that about one third of all the cocaine sold to young people is actually methamphetamine. When drug dealers

All prescribed medicines should be taken only as directed.

don't have enough cocaine, they often mix in methamphetamine or another stimulant. Crystal-meth is often substituted for crack cocaine. This leads to problems because the users get used to taking larger doses of the mixture. When they go back to straight cocaine, they may overdose.

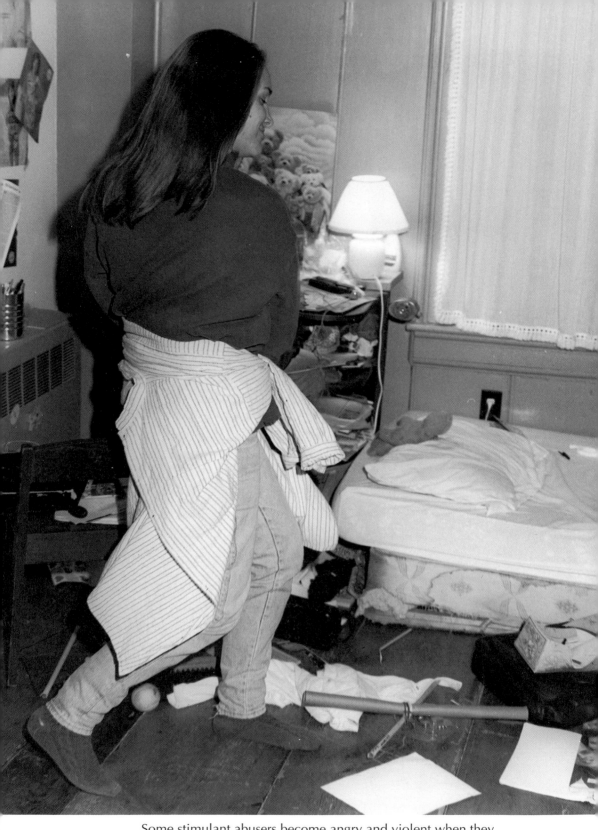

Some stimulant abusers become angry and violent when they are in withdrawal.

CHAPTER 2

Types of Stimulants

*S*timulants are drugs that speed up the mind and body. They make everything work faster, even the heart. Many users have died because their heart was beating so fast that it simply wore out.

There are many other dangers. Users may suffer from fever, convulsions, high blood pressure, depression, severe fatigue, intense anger, nausea, vomiting, stomach-ache, paranoia, blackouts, suicidal tendencies, coma, and death.

It is especially dangerous to use stimulants when exercising. Physical exertion causes the blood pressure and heart rate to increase. The stimulants have already increased the blood pressure and heart rate, so a stroke or heart attack can result.

14

Signs of stimulant use are enlarged pupils, sudden movements, impatience, anger, speed talking, dry mouth, periods of intense happiness, grinding of teeth, weight loss, increased alertness, inability to sleep, mood swings, loss of appetite, headaches, and chest pain. The long-term effects of using stimulants include a rash that looks like chickenpox, boils, gum disease, distorted vision, lung problems, uncontrolled shaking, and brain damage that results in loss of memory and ability to speak.

Going on a Run

People sometimes use stimulants over and over without stopping—even to sleep. Users call this "going on a run" or "tweekin'." When they do stop using, they "crash." They come down off the high. Then they become very angry, hostile, and depressed.

No one starts using stimulants expecting to become addicted (get "hooked"), be arrested ("busted"), or go into withdrawal (go "cold turkey"). But that is exactly what happens. Stimulants are extremely addictive. They are among the most abused drugs in the world.

Withdrawal

If people who are addicted to stimulants can't get drugs, they go into severe withdrawal. The signs of withdrawal include depression, paranoia, long periods of sleep, anger, constant hunger, lack of energy, occasional violence, and feeling absolutely terrible about yourself. This is one of the reasons that addicts will do almost anything to keep from being without the drug.

Withdrawal has a lot to do with crime. About 82 percent of all crime is drug-related. Addicts will do almost anything to get drugs. That includes robbery, burglary, writing bad checks, and shoplifting.

Many young people have been trapped by drugs, especially stimulants. Studies show that 66 percent of high school seniors have used an illegal drug. Over 60 percent of all addicts choose stimulants as their favorite drug.

Amphetamines

These drugs come in the form of pills, capsules, and tablets. The pills may be round or heart-shaped. They may be white, tan, pink, or green. The tablets are usually white and oval in shape. The

16 capsules are usually black and another color, clear, rust, or white. One capsule is green and clear.

Amphetamines are usually swallowed. They can be dissolved and injected into a vein. Sometimes they are crushed into powder and "snorted" up the nose.

They have many street names: "speed," "uppers," "pep pills," "hearts," "Black Beauties," "crosses," "bennies," "Mollies," "dexies," "dex," "truck drivers," "ups," "co-pilots," "footballs," and "go fast."

They also have trade names: Benzedrine, Dexedrine, Biphetamine, Metiatric, Obetrol, and Desoxyn.

Methamphetamine

This drug consists of methylamine and phenylpropanone. It is an extremely dangerous combination that is very hard to make. If it is made wrong, it becomes a deadly poison.

As mentioned in Chapter 1, most methamphetamine is made in illegal labs by people who are not trained. Because of this, the drugs they make often turn out wrong. Thousands of users have died of poorly made methamphetamine.

The drug has no known medical use. It comes in a white powder or rock form. In

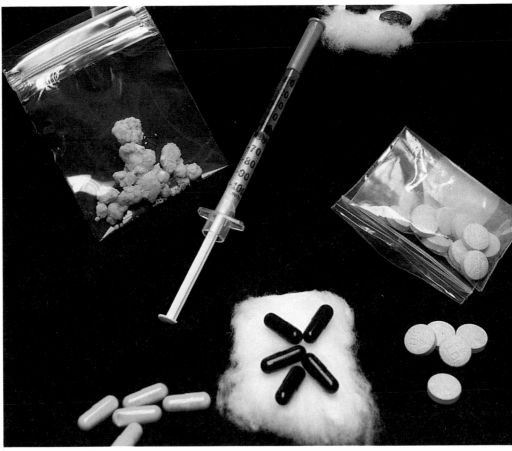

Stimulants are extremely addictive.

many ways it looks and acts like cocaine. Some dealers even sell it as cocaine.

It is extremely addictive. Some users report becoming hooked in less than two weeks. Street names for this drug include: "crystal," "go-fast," "meth," "crank," and "crystal-meth."

This drug is among the most abused of all the stimulants because it acts quickly. The high is almost instantaneous when it

17

18 is injected into a vein or snorted. It is called a "rush" because it is so powerful. The effects last from two to six hours.

Phenmetrazine

This drug comes only in pill form. It may be swallowed, crushed and snorted, or dissolved and injected into a vein.

Phenmetrazine is its medical name. It is prescribed by doctors to help people lose weight. On the street, you may hear it called "phen," "phenz," or "penny." The small pills can be round or square and white or pink and white.

Methylphenidate

A trade name of this drug is Ritalin. It is prescribed to calm hyperactive children.

When taken in large amounts, this drug acts very much like amphetamines. It is widely abused, especially by illegal aliens. In some countries methylphenidate can be bought over the counter. In the United States, it is only available by prescription.

The drug comes only in pill form. It is usually swallowed, although some users dilute it and inject it into a vein. The small, round pills may be yellow, pale yellow, or lime green. The street names for this drug include "rit," "pal," and "lin."

Other Stimulants

A few other stimulants are sometimes abused. They are just like amphetamines, except in chemical makeup.

The trade names for these drugs are Voranil, Plegine, Tenuate, Adipex, Cylert, Melfiat, Pre-Sate, Didrex, Prelu-2, Ionamin, Pondimin, and Tepanil. They are prescribed for control of hyperactive children and for cold symptoms and weight problems.

The street names for these drugs are "ten," "tennies," "two," "Pre," "Cy," "Mel," "Di," "Di-an," "Adi," "T," and "Yellows." Most users simply refer to these drugs as "speed."

These drugs come in several forms, but mostly in pills, tablets, and capsules. They must be swallowed, except that Cylert also comes in a chewable tablet, and Melfiat sometimes comes in liquid form.

They come in a variety of colors. The pills may be yellow, white, cream, cream with blue spots, tan, pale orange, pale green, gray, pink, or bright yellow. In tablet form, they are almost always white, but a few are tan. The capsules are usually two-toned, orange and white, dark green and light green, gray and yellow, or solid yellow.

Knowing the facts about drug abuse and addiction may save your life.

CHAPTER 3

The Truth About Stimulants

You hear a lot about drugs these days. Some of it is right. A lot of it isn't. The school tells you one thing. Your parents tell you another. Then your friends tell you something else. Like most teenagers, you've probably wondered what to believe about drugs. This chapter answers some of the questions asked by young people.

"What Is Addiction?"

Addiction is loss of control over use of a drug. Addicts are not able to control their drug use no matter how hard they try.

Many users become afraid that they are addicted. To prove that they are not, they try to stop using drugs for a while. This

22 usually works, especially for stimulant users, called "speed freaks." Even severely addicted stimulant users can stop using for a while. This is because all stimulant users quit long enough to crash.

There are some problems with this effort to find out if they are addicted, however.

The first problem is that they can't quit for good. They are too attracted to the high. So as soon as they have "proved" that they are not addicted, they start using the drugs again.

The second problem is that once they start using again, they can't tell how much they will use or how long the "run" will be. They may promise themselves to take only one "hit" or dose and stop. But when they start coming down, they want to go up again. The run may last for several days.

"Why Do People Become Addicts?"

Actually, many people don't *become* addicts. They are born with a tendency to become addicted. They inherit it the way they inherit the tendency to be tall or short, slim or fat. Some have such a strong tendency that they become addicted very quickly.

Addicts often turn to crime to support their habit.

24   There are two types of inherited addiction. One type goes from father or mother
to son or daughter. These addicts often
start using drugs in their late teens or
early twenties. They usually don't become
addicted until they have abused drugs for
several years.

The second type of inherited addiction
goes only from the father to the son.
These addicts may start using drugs very
early, frequently between the ages of 10
and 15. They lose control of their drug use
very quickly. They are also frequently violent when they are high. Within a few
years, these boys usually have criminal
records.

It works like this. Some people are
born with a tendency to make a brain
chemical called tetrohydroisoquinalin,
THIQ, for short. When they use a drug,
their brains make THIQ. The THIQ slows
down the manufacturing of the brain
chemicals that enable them to feel good.
This leaves them without any natural way
to feel good. So they use more drugs.

No one can tell if they have inherited a
tendency to make THIQ. So anyone who
decides to try drugs is taking a big risk.

Even if you did not inherit this tendency, you still can become addicted, but

it takes longer. Most people will become addicted if they use long enough. Stimulants are extremely addictive. Fewer than 10 percent of addicts ever quit.

"Do Addicts Always Die from Using Drugs?"

Almost always. Stimulants, like all drugs, kill addicts either directly or indirectly. Many stimulant addicts die as a direct result of using drugs. They die of overdose, heart attack, stroke, hemorrhage, or lung disease.

Stimulants also kill users in indirect ways. Drugs cause 45 percent of nonaccident hospital admissions, 50 percent of traffic deaths, 67 percent of suicide attempts, 33 percent of suicides, 86 percent of fire deaths, 65 percent of drownings, and 70 percent of fatal falls.

It really isn't a question of *whether* drugs will kill addicts. It is a question of *when* the drugs will kill them.

"What If I Use Drugs Only a Couple of Times?"

Lots of young people try this. Some actually do try them a few times and quit. Others continue until they are hooked.

Drugs produced in an illegal lab can be deadly poison.

Abusing stimulants, especially methamphetamine, is often fatal. This is so for many reasons. First, these drugs are made in illegal labs by untrained people. The chemicals used may be too old or too strong. They may be mixed or cooked incorrectly. They may have turned into a deadly poison.

Second, these drugs often contain other substances that are dangerous, even deadly. After the drugs leave the lab, they are given to a distributor. This person usually mixes the drug with some white powder. This is called "cutting," or "stepping on" the drug. Everything from baby laxatives to rat poison has been used to cut stimulants. The distributor then sells the drug to a dealer. The dealer cuts it again. This usually happens many times before the user finally gets the drug.

Third, sometimes a user buys the drug directly from the distributor, so it is almost pure. Drugs that have not been cut are so powerful that they often kill users.

Fourth, you may have a physical problem that makes drug use more dangerous for you than for others. You could be missing a certain blood chemical necessary to use cocaine. Or you could have a

28 weak heart or blood vessel that could break down.

Some people don't die the first time they use. It may be the second or the tenth or the fiftieth. With stimulants you can never be sure which drug experience will be your last.

"I'm Only Hurting Myself, So Who Cares?"

Drug use hurts everyone. It costs our country billions of dollars every year. We all pay for it—in hospital fees, insurance costs, taxes, and many other ways. Drug use also hurts our families. Family members tend to have more physical and emotional problems when someone they care about is addicted. Drug use causes 65 percent of child abuse, 82 percent of all crime, 50 percent of family violence, 75 percent of divorces, and 55 percent of runaways.

"If I Stop Using, Will Everything Be Okay?"

I wish the answer were a simple yes. It isn't. If you have been using stimulants for long, they may have done both mental and physical damage.

Drug abuse has ruined many lives.

30   Some of the damage done by stimulants can be cleared up after a long time. Some of it is permanent. Stimulants cause damage to the cells of the body. This can result in birth defects in your children.

You probably will need treatment as well. People who use stimulants develop personality problems that only a trained counselor can help with.

"What If I Am Addicted?"

You definitely need treatment! If possible, talk to your parents, teacher, school counselor, minister, priest, or rabbi. Ask them to help you get into treatment. If you can't, call (919) 781-9734. That is the number of the International Certification Reciprocity Consortium (ICRC). They can give you the number of a Certified Alcohol and Drug Counselor in almost any part of the United States or Canada or in the armed services.

CHAPTER 4

Why People Abuse Stimulants

*E*veryone from teenagers and parents to counselors and government officials has tried to understand why people abuse illegal drugs. There are a number of reasons. Each of them is discussed below.

"Because It Feels Good"

When people first try a stimulant, they get a rush. This is an intense feeling of pleasure. They feel happy, powerful, smart, and full of energy. They may stay high for days. Stimulant abusers like this feeling so much that they take the drug over and over. Taking a drug because it feels good is sometimes called psychological addiction.

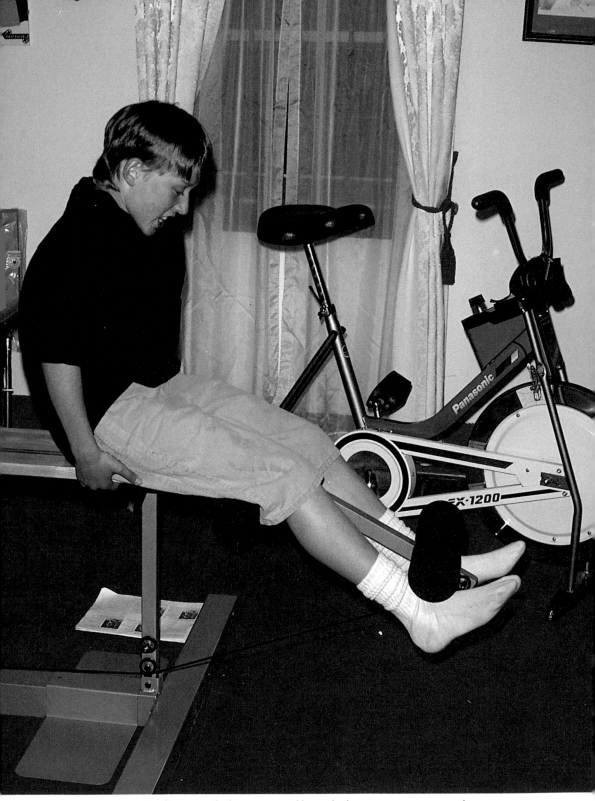

Feeling good about yourself can help you to stay away from drugs.

A major problem with stimulants is that *33* they destroy the part of the liver that processes the drug. So the abuser must keep increasing the amount of stimulant to get high. This condition is called tolerance. It is very dangerous.

All stimulants will kill if taken in large enough doses. So each time addicts increase the dose, they are getting closer to the amount that will kill them.

"Because It Runs in Our Family"

There are several reasons why addiction runs in families. Drug use may be considered normal. In some families everyone, or almost everyone, abuses drugs. Parents may supply their teenagers or leave the drugs where the teens can get them.

Drug abuse may be the family's way of coping with problems. Some families never talk about or solve problems. Instead, they find that drug use seems to make them forget their problems. Of course, it really makes things worse. Now they have all the same problems plus drug addiction.

Finally, some addiction is inherited from the father or the mother, as was discussed in Chapter 3.

34 | *"Because Dealers 'Push' Them"*

Some people get addicted to drugs because dealers (sometimes called "pushers") pressure them. The dealers are very good at that. They can make you feel stupid or weak if you don't try drugs.

Dealers have many ways to get teens hooked on drugs. It is their job. They may threaten to hurt you or someone you care about. They may give you free samples. They will do whatever they can to get you hooked. Once you're addicted, they know you'll buy again and again.

"Because I Was in Pain"

Some people become addicted after being injured or having surgery. Their doctor prescribes medication to help them deal with the pain. As they recover, the doctor begins reducing the amount of medication. At that point, some people turn to illegal drugs to avoid the pain.

What they don't realize is that pain can be both bad and good. Bad pain happens when a person is injured. It serves as a warning. If you burn your hand, the bad pain warns you to move your hand. While you are recovering from an accident, the good pain lets you know that healing is

Drug abusers are out of control and may resort to stealing from their own family.

36 taking place. It usually goes away as you get better. It is better to learn to live with some pain than to become addicted.

"Because of Emotional Pain"

Some people start using stimulants because they are depressed. Maybe they have broken up with a boyfriend or girl-friend. Perhaps they aren't happy with how they look. Maybe they didn't make the football team or the cheerleading squad. Whatever the reason, these people are in emotional pain.

They started using stimulants to help them feel better. But stimulants only work for a short time. When the high wears off, they feel much worse than they did in the beginning. Now, of course, they have a real problem, drug addiction.

"Because of Peer Pressure"

One of the most common reasons given by kids who are addicted to drugs is, "Everyone else was doing it." Many addicts will try to get you to use drugs. Here are some of the reasons why:

• Most addicts get their drugs by supplying their friends. They buy a quantity of drugs on credit. Then they either cut it or double the price. They sell half to friends and pay off the dealer with the profit. So the half they use is free.

- If users can get their friends to use drugs, it makes them feel normal. Kids who are addicted feel and act strange. They see that others are normal. That makes them feel worse. If they can get their normal friends to use, they feel better about being addicted.

- They gain power over you. Kids who use drugs feel absolutely powerless because of their addiction. The addiction has control. It tells them what to do. Often they would like to quit using drugs, but they can't do it on their own. The drugs are too powerful. Since they can't control their addiction, they look for something they *can* control. If they can get you to use drugs, they control you. That makes them feel powerful.

Long-term use of stimulants can change your thinking and your sense of reality.

CHAPTER 5

What Stimulants Do to Your Mind

*A*ll mood-altering drugs affect how your mind works, but stimulants do it in very special ways. Most of the ways are very painful. The longer you use stimulants, the more pain you will have.

It is important to understand this. Don't be fooled by the good feeling you get soon after using these drugs. As soon as they begin to wear off, *the pain will come*.

Stimulants trick your mind into believing or feeling something that is not real. Let's look at this a little more closely.

Energy

The first trick is that stimulants make you feel as if you have more energy than you do. When you first use a stimulant,

40 you work and play much harder than usual. You find it hard to hold still. You may even have trouble not talking.

When the stimulant begins to wear off, you start feeling very tired. Your muscles are sore. You won't want to talk, even to people you care about. You used up most of your real energy because of the false feeling of energy that the drug gave you.

Sleep

Stimulants trick you into thinking that you are not sleepy. It is not unusual for stimulant addicts to stay awake for a week without ever feeling sleepy. As a matter of fact, most people using stimulants can't force themselves to go to sleep.

When they quit using stimulants, they crash. They feel very sleepy. They may sleep for days. Even in an emergency, they often cannot stay awake.

Appetite

Stimulant use makes you believe that you are not hungry. Many users eat very little or nothing at all for several days. Of course, this causes them to lose weight. Many addicts say they use the drug to control their weight.

As soon as they stop using the stimulant, however, they are very hungry. They start eating huge amounts of food. They usually gain back all of the weight they lost, plus a few pounds.

Happiness

While stimulant users are high, they feel very happy. The drug makes them think that everything is wonderful. They feel great about themselves. They believe that they are smart, beautiful, and able to do almost anything they want to do.

When they crash, they become depressed. They feel miserable. They hate themselves and the way they look. They feel stupid and unable to do anything right. Many of them feel so worthless and hopeless that they attempt suicide.

Peace

Some stimulant users say that they experience times of great peace. They feel that everything is right with the world.

Other users become very hostile. They are rude, even to their friends. They often become aggressive and frightening to others. Many of them become violent. Some seriously injure or even kill others.

42 | ### Trust

When stimulant users are high, they may trust anyone. They lend money to people without even thinking about it. They let people they hardly know drive their cars or sleep in their homes.

But if they use too much of the drug, they become paranoid (suspicious). They think people are staring at them, or following them, or talking about them.

Bravery

When people are using, they are afraid of nothing. They may fight people much bigger and stronger. They may drive cars very fast and dangerously. They take chances that would frighten the ordinary person. Some have continued to fight with police even after having been shot several times.

However, these same people easily go into a panic when they crash. They may be afraid of people much smaller and younger. They may be afraid to drive a car. A loud noise may make them jump and perhaps run away.

Reality

While using stimulants, most people say that they are able to think very clearly.

It's common for stimulant abusers to have a huge appetite when they stop taking drugs.

44 They say that they can easily solve difficult problems. They believe that they see the world as it actually is.

When they get too much of the drug, however, they have hallucinations. They believe these imagined things are real. Often they believe bugs are crawling on their bodies or that a monster is about to eat them.

Sociability

Stimulant users who are high may be very sociable. They act overly friendly. They may talk to complete strangers for hours. Some users have sex with people they don't even like.

When these people crash, they usually want to be left alone. They may lock themselves in their room and pull the shades. They may take the phone off the hook or refuse to answer it if it rings.

These are some of the ways that stimulants damage your mind. If you use them very long, you will begin to have trouble knowing what is real. You may not even know what you feel.

Long-term stimulant abusers will have most, if not all, of the problems discussed in this chapter. If you use stimulants at all, you will have some of them.

CHAPTER 6

How Your Stimulant Use Affects Your Family

 We've discussed the damage that stimulant use can do to you. It can also harm your family.

Having an addicted person in the family is very painful for other members because they care about the addict. The addict, however, cannot really relate to anyone anymore. The drugs get in the way.

To deal with the hurt, family members sometimes relate in abnormal ways. These ways are called "family roles." Research shows that there are many of these roles. We will discuss some of them here.

45

46 | ## The Dependent

This is the person who is actually addicted to a drug. He or she behaves in ways that are very painful for the other family members. They won't talk about their feelings because they are in pain.

The Chief Enabler

This is the person whose behavior allows the dependent to remain on drugs. It could be a parent or a brother or sister. The chief enabler does things like writing excuses when the addict has missed school, bailing the addict out of jail, giving the addict money, or lying to the police. The chief enabler usually does care about the dependent's drug use, but wants to help. The problem is that the "helping" allows the dependent to stay hooked.

The Hero

The hero is the family member who tries to take the attention off the dependent by doing everything well. This person may be a star athlete or an honor student. It is hard to do everything well, and the hero may suffer from trying. These teens seldom get the help they need because others don't see that they need it.

It can be very painful for a child to see his or her parents abuse drugs.

The Rebel

This person responds to the dependent's addiction by getting into trouble. Rebels may be in so much trouble that the rest of the family do not even notice the dependent's problem. It is usually less painful for parents to deal with a child who is stealing or fighting than with one who is addicted.

The Lost Child

This person responds to the family pain by withdrawing. It is often a younger brother or sister. The lost child cannot stand what is happening to the family. He or she tries to make no demands so that no more stress is added.

The Mascot

Mascots deal with the pain by trying to be as cute and lovable as possible. It is as if they are saying, "I will make up for the problem by being so cute you will never even notice that someone we love is killing himself or herself with drugs."

The Blamer

Blamers try to take the focus off the ad-dict by pointing the finger at other family members or situations. They say things like, "If you were any kind of a father, you would earn more money. Then [the dependent] would be happier," or, "How can you blame him? He has had it pretty tough since YOU divorced Dad."

The Placater

Placaters try to deal with the family pain by assuring other family members that everything is just fine with the addict. They say things like, "He is just being a kid. All kids get depressed sometimes," or "I was pretty angry as a kid myself; this is just normal behavior."

The Martyr

Martyrs try to take the focus off the dependent by drawing family attention to themselves. They do this by always giving to others and never getting. They say things like, "I was going to be a nurse, but I think I'll put that off for a couple of years. You need help around here."

The Peacemaker

Peacemakers never let others have a disagreement, not to mention a fight. They are constantly on guard to stop any

50 conflict. With a peacemaker in the family, conflicts are seldom settled. The addict's drug problem is not even discussed, so there is never a chance to get professional help for the addict or the family.

The Distractor

Distractors do things to stop any conversation about the dependent's drug problem. They change the subject, fall down, or say, "You scare me when you use that tone of voice."

The Clown

Clowns use humor to keep the family from focusing on the dependent's behavior. Whenever a family member raises an issue that might reveal the addict's problem, the clown starts joking. It is sometimes hard to realize that while clowns joke and laugh, they are in pain.

Irrelevant One

Irrelevant ones bring up things that are not under discussion to be sure that there is no possibility of the addict's problem coming up. As always, the goal is to guard against the real family pain, that of living with an addict.

The Therapist

Therapists try to help other family members solve their problems. This causes the others to concentrate on their own problems. That way, no one has a chance to realize that the family's real problem is living with an addict.

The Tyrant

Tyrants try to make everyone in the family do exactly as they say. This causes a lot of resentment. It also makes each member secretly support the addict's rebellion against the tyrant. So the addiction just gets worse.

The Scapegoat

Scapegoats deal with family pain by pretending that they caused it. When this happens, the other family members dump all the blame on the scapegoat. That means that no one deals with the addict's problem, so the situation only gets worse.

It is important to remember that no family has all these roles. Also some family members can play several roles.

You may be surprised at how much pain your drug use can cause other family members. Addiction is painful for everyone in the family.

Most teens are introduced to drugs by their friends.

CHAPTER 7

Avoiding Peer Pressure

*M*any experts believe that peer pressure is the major reason young people get hooked on drugs. Your "peers" are others of your age. "Peer pressure" means trying to make you do something. Peer pressure can be good or bad. For our purposes, it means pressure to use drugs.

Desire to Be Liked

Everyone wants to be liked. You feel good when people like you. Most teenagers want to be popular. You are in a very social stage of life. You need to learn how to get along with others. The things you learn now affect the rest of your life. Good social skills may help you be successful when you become an adult.

53

54
But bad peer pressure can lead to your becoming pregnant, contracting AIDS, or getting hooked on drugs.

Wanting to Be "Cool," "Bad," "Radical," "Awesome"

The words change, but the idea is that you want the other kids to respect you.

But where does respect come from? It starts with self-respect. Would you respect someone who didn't respect himself or herself?

Do you respect people who use drugs? Would others respect you if you used drugs? How would you feel about yourself if you become addicted?

Fear of Criticism

Let's face it, no one likes being criticized. Being made fun of can be painful.

But what do teens think of those who use drugs? Do they make friends of the speed freaks, the "stoners"? Or do they criticize them?

Being Part of the Group

Sure you want to belong. Everyone wants that. Being part of a group is fun. It means that you are accepted.

Staying away from drugs doesn't mean you can't have a good time.

Look around. Do your classmates or friends who use drugs accept people for who they are? Or do they accept only people who use drugs? If it depends on whether or not you're a user, do they care more about you or about drugs?

Look around some more. What about the group who don't use drugs? Which group seems to have the most fun? Which group would you trust? Yes, being a part of a group is important. Just be sure you pick the right one!

56 | ## *Beating Peer Pressure*

We have talked about why peer pressure can be hard for you. Now let's look at ways you can beat peer pressure.

Know yourself. It is important to have a sense of who you are. Psychologists call this "a sense of identity." It means knowing what you want out of life. Do you want to be an airline pilot, an army officer, or a senator?

Drugs could ruin your chance to be any of those things. If you know who you are and what you want, it will be hard for anyone to push you into taking drugs.

Have a long-range view. That means seeing the big picture. Have you ever seen a movie about someone's life? If you could see a movie of how things were going to turn out for you, would it affect the way you live today? Of course it would!

If you knew that your first child would be born retarded because you had used drugs when you were 14, would you use them anyway? If you knew that you would become permanently paralyzed after a bad dose of drugs, would you continue to use them? If you knew that drugs would kill parts of your brain every time you used them, would you go on?

If you have a long-range view, you can
see that using drugs hurts your chances
of success in life. Counselors often refer
to addicts as "chronic underachievers."
This means that they never get as far as
they could have.

Be assertive. This means telling people
what you want and what you do not want.
It means saying no and meaning it. It
means refusing to use drugs or ending
your use. Assertiveness can be difficult at
first, but it gets easier with practice.

When you first use assertiveness, drug
dealers will try to make you give in. If you
continue to say no, they will leave you
alone.

Ask an adult's advice. Parents and
other adults can help you find ways to deal
with peer pressure. Pastors, rabbis, teach-
ers, grandparents have had years of
experience in dealing with things like peer
pressure. (Yes, they had problems with
peer pressure even then.) You may be surprised how well their advice works.

It is important that you make up your
own mind about drug use. Don't let someone else decide for you. Resisting peer
pressure means that *you* get to decide.

Glossary

Explaining New Words

abuse Use of a drug in a manner other than that prescribed.

addiction State or condition of being unable to stop using a drug.

cold turkey Suddenly stopping the use of a drug without medical help.

coma Unconsciousness.

convulsion Involuntary and violent spasm of the muscles.

copilots Truck drivers' slang for stimulants.

crash The depression that hits stimulant abusers when coming down from a high.

crystal–meth Street name for combination of methedrine and amphetamine; also called methamphetamine.

detox Process of stopping drug use.

dose Amount of a drug used at one time.

drop To take a drug by mouth.

genetic tendency An inborn condition of being prone to something; in this book, being born prone to addiction.

run Period of several days of drug use without sleep.

seizure A spasm of the body.

speed Slang for drugs that excite the mind and body.

speedball A combination of speed and heroin.

speed talking Rapid, nonstop talking often done by persons high on speed.

stash An addict's supply of drugs.

step on To mix a nondrug into a drug.

THIQ (tetrahydroisoquinalin) A chemical found in the brains of both alcoholics and cocaine addicts. It is believed to suppress the chemicals that give a sense of peace and well-being.

tweekin' Another term for "going on a run." Using stimulants over and over without stopping.

uppers Drugs that excite the mind and body; also called *speed*.

withdrawal The physical effects of being without drugs.

Help List

Alcoholics Anonymous World Service, Inc.
P.O. Box 459, Grand Central Station
New York, NY 10163
(212) 586-8700

American Council for Drug Education
204 Monroe Street
Rockville, MD 20852
(301) 294–0600

International Certification Reciprocity Consortium
3725 National Drive
Raleigh, NC 27612
(919) 781–9734

Narcotics Anonymous World Service Office
16155 Wyandotte Street
Van Nuys, CA 91406

(818) 780–3951

National Association of Children of Alcoholics
31706 Pacific Coast Highway
South Laguna, CA 95677
(713) 499–3889

National Clearinghouse for Alcohol and Drug Information
P.O. Box 2345
Rockville, MD 20852
(301) 468–2600

National Council on Alcoholism and Drug Dependency
12 West 21st Street
New York, NY 10010
(800) 662–HELP

National Federation of Drug–Free Youth
8730 Georgia Avenue
Silver Springs, MD 20910
(800) 554–5437

National Prevention Network
444 North Capitol Street NW
Washington, DC 20001

For Further Reading

Ball. J. *Everything You Need to Know about Drug Abuse*, rev. ed. New York: Rosen Publishing Group, 1994.

Berger, G. *The Pressure to Take Drugs.* New York: Franklin Watts, 1990.

Clayton, L. *Barbiturates and Other Depressants.* New York: Rosen Publishing Group, 1994.

Clayton, L. *Designer Drugs.* New York: Rosen Publishing Group, 1993.

Latson, E. *Old Patterns, New Truths.* New York: Harper/Hazelden, 1989.

Leite, E., and Espeland, P. *Different Like Me.* Minneapolis: Johnson Institute, 1987.

Levy, S. *Managing the Drugs in Your Life.* New York: McGraw–Hill, 1989.

McFarland, R. *Coping with Substance Abuse.* New York: Rosen Publishing Group, 1990.

Porterfield, K. *Coping with an Alcoholic Parent.* New York: Rosen Publishing Group, 1991.

Index

About the Author

Dr. Lawrence Clayton earned his doctorate from Texas Woman's University. He is an ordained minister and has served as such since 1972. Dr. Clayton is a clinical marriage and family therapist and certified drug and alcohol counselor. He is also president of the Oklahoma Professional Drug and Alcohol Conselor's Certification Board. Dr. Clayton lives with his wife, Cathy, and their three children in Piedmont, Oklahoma.

Photo Credits

Cover photo: Stuart Rabinowitz
Page 17: ©Greg Smith/Gamma-Liaison; p. 20: ©Alice Q. Hargrave/Gamma-Liaison; pp. 23, 26: Gamma-Liaison; p.29: ©Jean Marc Giboux/Gamma-Liaison; all other photos: Staurt Rabinowitz.

Design & Production: Blackbirch Graphics, Inc.